I Belong to the Muslim Faith

Katie Dicker and Zohal Azizi

PowerKiDS
press.

New York

Published in 2010 by The Rosen Publishing Group Inc.
29 East 21st Street, New York, NY 10010

First Edition

Library of Congress Cataloging-in-Publication Data

Dicker, Katie.
  I belong to the Muslim faith / Katie Dicker and Zoha Azizi.
     p. cm. -- (I belong)
  Includes index.
  ISBN 978-1-4358-3035-6 (library binding)
  ISBN 978-1-4358-8624-7 (paperback)
  ISBN 978-1-4358-8625-4 (6-pack)
  1. Islam--Juvenile literature. I. Azizi, Zoha. II. Title.
  BP161.3.D563 2010
  297—dc22

                                    2008051878

Manufactured in China

Disclaimer
The text in this book is based on the experience of one family. Although every effort
has been made to offer accurate and clearly expressed information, the author and
publisher acknowledge that some explanations may not be relevant to those who
practice their faith in a different way.

Acknowledgements
The author and publisher would like to thank the following people for their help and
participation in this book:
The Azizi family, Bindu Rai, and Mohammad Hoda.

Photography by Chris Fairclough.

Contents

A celebration

Hi, I'm Zohal. Today it's **Eid-ul-Fitr** and my family are celebrating the end of **Ramadan**. We're Muslims—we follow the religion of Islam. Last night, there was a new moon, which meant that Eid-ul-Fitr could begin.

I've come to the **mosque** with my dad and my brothers, to thank **Allah** for helping us **fast** during Ramadan.

The mosque is really busy today. Everyone is gathering outside before we go in to **pray**. Tents have been put up beside the mosque so there is space for everyone.

This man is giving money to help the poor. We share the things that Allah has given us, especially during Ramadan.

At the mosque

We can go to the mosque every day, but Friday is a special day for Muslims. Just after noon, men gather at the mosque to say the Friday prayer called Jumu'ah.

The mosque is a short drive from our house. It has two prayer halls and smaller rooms, where we can meet with our friends.

We go to the mosque to **worship** Allah with other Muslims. Allah created the world and looks after us. It makes me happy to think of all the good things that Allah has given me.

We take off our shoes before we go into the mosque, because we want to keep it clean. It's also to show our respect for Allah.

Salat

Muslims pray five times a day—at dawn, noon, in the afternoon, at sunset, and just before bed. These prayers are called Salat. We say our prayers at home or at the mosque.

Men and women worship in different halls at the mosque. But wherever we pray, we all face toward **Mecca**.

The prayer halls are very large. There are no pictures or statues that might distract us—we only think about Allah when we pray. We praise Allah our creator, and ask for his help in our lives.

These clocks show the times of Salat and the Friday prayer. The times change each day, depending on the position of the sun.

How do we pray?

There are four main positions of prayer. We stand up so that Allah can hear what we are saying, then we kneel and bow to show our respect. Finally, we touch our hands and our head to the ground.

We pray in a language called Arabic. During our prayers, we say *Allaho-Akbar*, which means "Allah is great."

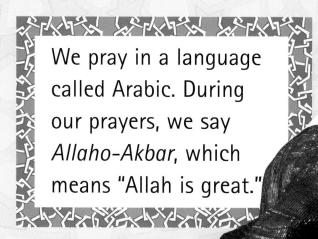

Before we pray, we wash our hands and our face. It's important to be clean and pure in what we say and do, whenever we worship Allah. We use prayer mats so we don't have to touch the floor.

We all face toward Mecca when we pray at home, just like we do at the mosque.

Who was Muhammad?

Muhammad (peace be upon him) was
a **prophet**. He was born in Mecca
nearly 1,500 years ago. Every time
we mention his name, we say "peace
be upon him (pbuh)" to show
our respect for him.

The **imam** leads
the prayers at
the mosque. He
shows us how to
follow the Islamic
way of life, as
the prophets
did long ago.

The prophets taught people about the wonders of Allah and passed on his wisdom. Allah's teachings are written in our holy book, the **Qur'an** or Koran. His words were given to Muhammad (pbuh) by the angel Gabriel, Allah's messenger.

The Qur'an is full of beautiful rhyming verses. When I read the Qur'an, I put it on a wooden stand to keep it safe and clean.

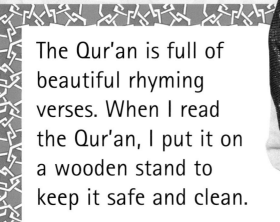

13

My guide to life

The Qur'an is written in Arabic. Dad helps me to understand what the words mean. The Qur'an teaches us how important it is to obey Allah. Allah's words also remind me of the power of goodness over evil.

When I'm unsure of something, I turn to the Qur'an to guide me. It's comforting to hear Allah's words.

I wear a scarf called a hijab each day as a sign of **modesty.** I also follow sayings called Hadith. These words describe the way Muhammad (pbuh) followed Allah's teachings in his life.

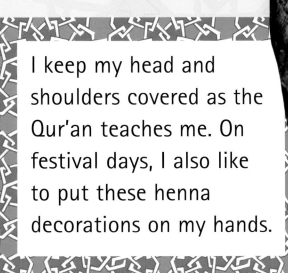

I keep my head and shoulders covered as the Qur'an teaches me. On festival days, I also like to put these henna decorations on my hands.

Helping others

Allah has sent angels to watch over and record my deeds. One day, Allah will choose whether I go to **heaven** when I die. I try to have good manners and to behave as Allah has taught me.

I often help Dad with the shopping—it's good to lend a hand. We've been to this shop to buy halal meat.

At school, I was asked to be a counselor. People in my class come to see me if they're worried about something. I'm good at listening and I try to make them feel better.

Allah teaches us to be kind and thoughtful to others. I try to follow Allah's guidance every day.

Food and fasting

The Qur'an says we shouldn't eat or drink when it is daylight during the month of Ramadan. Being hungry and thirsty teaches us to control our feelings and to be grateful for what we have.

During Ramadan, we think of other people who do not have enough to eat. Our dinner tastes very good when we've been fasting!

The Qur'an also says we're not allowed to eat some foods. We don't eat pork or any animals that eat meat, or have not been slaughtered in the name of Allah. This is because the Qur'an says they're unclean.

We describe foods as halal or haram. We can eat halal food, but the Qur'an says haram food is unlawful.

Muslim festivals

At Eid-ul-Fitr, we celebrate the end of the fast that we have all shared together. Over this three-day festival, lots of friends and family will visit us.

On festival days, we have a special meal and share sweet foods to bring everyone a sweet time ahead.

At **Eid-ul-Adha** we think about how
we should obey Allah's teachings.
We remember that the prophet
Abraham (pbuh) was willing
to sacrifice his son for Allah.
This festival comes at the
end of the **Hajj**.

I wear this dress
to make me feel
special on festival
days. Some of the
threads are made
from real silver!

Glossary, further information, and Web Sites

Allah an Arabic name for God.

fast to go without food.

Hajj a special journey when Muslims try to visit Mecca as a sign of respect to Allah.

heaven the place where Muslims believe they will go to live when they die.

imam a person who leads Muslim worship.

Mecca a place in Saudi Arabia where the prophet Muhammad was born.

modesty to dress in a way that does not show off parts of the body.

mosque a building where Muslims go to worship Allah.

pray to talk to God. Muslims pray to Allah to give thanks, or to ask for help or forgiveness.

prophet a messenger sent by God.

Qur'an a special book full of Allah's words. Also called the Koran.

Ramadan a month of fasting during daylight hours.

worship to show love and respect to Allah.

Did you know?

- Islam began in Saudi Arabia almost 1,500 years ago.
- The word *Islam* means "peace."
- There are over one billion Muslims today, mostly living in the Middle East, Asia, and North Africa.
- There are two main groups in the Muslim religion, called Sunnis and Shiites.
- The dates of Muslim festivals follow a lunar calendar.

Activities

1. Plan to visit a local mosque. Write down all the things you can see. Which way is the direction of Mecca?
2. Find the location of Mecca on a map. Research using books or the internet to find out why Mecca is so important to Muslims.
3. Draw a design for a prayer mat using Muslim symbols.

Books to read

- *Islam for Children* by Ahmad Von Denffer (Islamic Foundation, 2007)

- *Ramadhan and Id-ul-Fitr* by Azra Jessa (Tahrike Tarsile Qur'an, 2008)

- *Rookie Read-About Holidays: Ramadan* by David F Marx (Children's Press, 2002)

- *This is my Faith: Islam* by Anita Ganeri (Barrons Educational, 2006)

Web Sites

Due to the changing nature of Internet links, PowerKids Press has developed an online list of Web sites related to the subject of this book. This site is updated regularly. Please use this link to access this list: www.powerkidslinks.com/blong/muslim

Muslim festivals

Al Hijra (December/January)
The Islamic New Year.

Mawlid (February/March)
The birthday of the prophet Muhammad.

Eid-ul-Fitr (October)
A three-day festival to end the fast of Ramadan.

Eid-ul-Adha (December/January)
A three-day festival when Muslims remember that the prophet Abraham was willing to sacrifice his son for Allah.

Muslim symbols

Star and crescent the moon and star are used as a symbol of the way that Islam guides and lights a Muslim's way through life.

Arabic script some Arabic words are used as a symbol of Islam. The word for "Allah," for example, is often used as a decoration in Muslim books and pictures.

Index